5/11

6 15
Lexile: _____

AR/BL: _____

AR Points: _____

# Environment

## in FOCUS

# Ecological Footprints

Cheryl Jakab

**Marshall Cavendish**
Benchmark

New York

This edition first published in 2011 in the United States of America by
Marshall Cavendish Benchmark
An imprint of Marshall Cavendish Corporation

Website: www.marshallcavendish.us

This publication represents the opinions and views of the author based on Cheryl Jakab's personal experience, knowledge, and research. The information in this book serves as a general guide only. The author and publisher have used their best efforts in preparing this book and disclaim liability rising directly and indirectly from the use and application of this book.

Other Marshall Cavendish Offices:
Marshall Cavendish International (Asia) Private Limited, 1 New Industrial Road, Singapore 536196 • Marshall Cavendish International (Thailand) Co Ltd. 253 Asoke, 12th Flr, Sukhumvit 21 Road, Klongtoey Nua, Wattana, Bangkok 10110, Thailand • Marshall Cavendish (Malaysia) Sdn Bhd, Times Subang, Lot 46, Subang Hi-Tech Industrial Park, Batu Tiga, 40000 Shah Alam, Selangor Darul Ehsan, Malaysia

Marshall Cavendish is a trademark of Times Publishing Limited

All websites were available and accurate when this book was sent to press.

Library of Congress Cataloging-in-Publication Data

Jakab, Cheryl.
  Ecological footprints / Cheryl Jakab.
    p. cm. — (Environment in focus)
  Includes index.
  Summary: "Discusses the environmental issue of large ecological footprints and how to create a sustainable way of living"—Provided by publisher.
  ISBN 978-1-60870-088-2
  1. Nature—Effect of human beings on—Juvenile literature. 2. Human ecology—Juvenile literature. 3. Sustainable living—Juvenile literature. I. Title.
  GF75.J36 2011
  304.2—dc22
                        2009042297

First published in 2010 by
MACMILLAN EDUCATION AUSTRALIA PTY LTD
15–19 Claremont Street, South Yarra 3141

Visit our website at www.macmillan.com.au or go directly to www.macmillanlibrary.com.au

Associated companies and representatives throughout the world.

Edited by Margaret Maher
Text and cover design by Cristina Neri, Canary Graphic Design
Page layout by Domenic Lauricella
Photo research by Sarah Johnson
Illustrations by Domenic Lauricella
Maps courtesy of Geo Atlas

Printed in the United States

**Acknowledgments**
The author and the publisher are grateful to the following for permission to reproduce copyright material:

Front cover photograph: An expansive green hillside overlooking downtown Houston, Texas, © David Huntely/Shutterstock.

Image copyright © Carbon Heroes, 15; © Andy Aitchison/CORBIS, 22; Graph adapted from Footprint Network, www.footprintnetwork.org, 24; Image copyright © Global Footprint Network, 29; © iStockphoto, 6 (bottom), 13; © Rüdiger Geis/iStockphoto, 12; © Andrew_Howe/iStockphoto, 28; © LattaPictures/iStockphoto, 26; © Matthew Palmer/iStockphoto, 10; © Terraxplorer/iStockphoto, 20; Image copyright © Mia McDonald, The Greenbelt Movement, 19; © Jeremy Woodhouse/Masterfile, 7 (middle), 25; RAF MAKDA/Photolibrary, 27; Science Photo Library/Photolibrary, 18; © AND Inc/Shutterstock, 11; © Natalia Bratslavsky/Shutterstock, 16; © Terrance Emerson/Shutterstock, 14; © haider/Shutterstock, 7 (top), 21; © Monkey Business Images/Shutterstock, 6 (top), 9; © mushin44/Shutterstock, 23; © Photoroller/Shutterstock, 5; © urosr/Shutterstock, 7 (bottom), 17; © A.S Zain/Shutterstock, 8.

**Please note**
At the time of printing, the Internet addresses appearing in this book were correct. Owing to the dynamic nature of the Internet, however, we cannot guarantee that all these addresses will remain correct.

1 3 5 6 4 2

# Contents

**Glossary Words**
When a word is printed in **bold**, you can look up its meaning in the glossary on page 31.

# Environment in Focus

**Hi there!** This is Earth speaking. Will you spare a moment to listen to me? I have some very important things to discuss.

We must focus on to some urgent environmental problems! All living things depend on my environment, but the way you humans are living at the moment, I will not be able to keep looking after you.

The issues I am worried about are:

- large ecological footprints
- damage to natural wonders
- widespread pollution in the environment
- the release of **greenhouse gases** into the **atmosphere**
- poor management of waste
- environmental damage caused by food production

My challenge to you is to find a **sustainable** way of living. Read on to find out what people around the world are doing to try to help.

## Fast Fact

Concerned people in local, national, and international groups are trying to understand how our way of life causes environmental problems. This important work helps us learn how to live more sustainably now and in the future.

# What's the Issue?
## Large Ecological Footprints

Ecological footprints are a way of describing resource use. The size of our ecological footprints depends on how much land is needed to provide everything we use and to treat the waste we produce.

Ecological footprints are measured in units called global acres. One global acre is an acre with a productivity equal to the world's average productivity.

## Our Ecological Footprint

Today, our ecological footprint is estimated to be larger than the area of productive land, or **biocapacity**, available. Across the world, people need to reduce their ecological footprints to sustainable levels. This means that each person would need to have an ecological footprint of 4.4 global acres (1.8 global hectares) or less. We can achieve this by reducing the amount of resources we use and reducing the amount of waste we produce.

## Resource Use

Almost all the resources we use come from the earth, including most of our energy and all of our food. Today, our total resource use is well beyond the amount that Earth can sustain.

*Building large homes and using a lot of electricity increases people's ecological footprints.*

# Ecological Footprint Issues

The most urgent ecological footprint issues around the globe include:

- lifestyles with very large resource demands
- the increase in carbon footprints
- the unequal sharing of resources
- the increasing size of national ecological footprints
- the **consumption** of more resources than Earth's biocapacity can provide

ARCTIC OCEAN

Arctic Circle

NORTH AMERICA

United States

NORTH ATLANTIC OCEAN

Equator

Brazil

SOUTH AMERICA

## ISSUE 1

**United States**
Some lifestyles are using more resources than Earth can supply. See pages 8–11.

## Fast Fact
The Worldwatch Institute says that the world's armed forces are most likely the single largest polluter on Earth.

## ISSUE 2

**Brazil**
Clearing forests is increasing carbon footprints.
See pages 12–15.

# Around the Globe

## ISSUE 4

**Dubai**
Luxury lifestyles are increasing national footprints. See pages 20–23.

EUROPE

A S I A

Japan

Dubai

AFRICA

NORTH

PACIFIC

*Tropic of Cancer*

OCEAN

## ISSUE 3

**Africa**
Many people are living without equal access to resources.
See pages 16–19.

## ISSUE 5

**Japan**
Japan's resources cannot be supplied by its available land, causing ecological overshoot.
See pages 24–27.

# Big Resource Demands

Some people's lifestyles have very large resource demands. Modern lifestyles in **developed countries** are based on huge resource consumption in homes and industry.

## Calculating Footprints

A person's ecological footprint is calculated by adding up all the food, energy, goods, and services he or she uses. The more a person consumes, the bigger his or her ecological footprint. Buying lots of goods, traveling in large cars, and using lots of energy creates large ecological footprints.

## Energy from Fossil Fuels

Most of the energy used across the world for electricity and transportation comes from burning **fossil fuels**. When fossil fuels are burned, they release greenhouse gases, including **carbon dioxide**, that lead to **global warming**. Greenhouse gases make up about half of the biggest ecological footprints. This is because biocapacity is needed to absorb these gases.

### Fast Fact
The part of an ecological footprint that is created by greenhouse gas **emissions** is sometimes called a carbon footprint.

*The use of fossil fuels, such as coal, makes up a large part of developed countries' big footprints.*

*The resources used to process, package, and import foods increase the size of ecological footprints.*

## CASE STUDY
# The United States' Footprint

In 2005, the average footprint per person in the United States was 24 global acres (9.7 global ha). The United States has about 5 percent of the world's population. However, it consumes as much as 25 percent of the energy produced in the world.

## Reasons the United States Has a Large Footprint

The large U.S. footprint comes from heavy use of modern conveniences. These include large cars, central heating, and electric appliances, which are powered by fossil fuels. One of the main contributors to the U.S. footprint is the oil used for transportation. Consumption of large amounts of meat and processed, packaged, and **imported** foods also increases the average footprint. This is because large amounts of resources are needed to produce and transport these products.

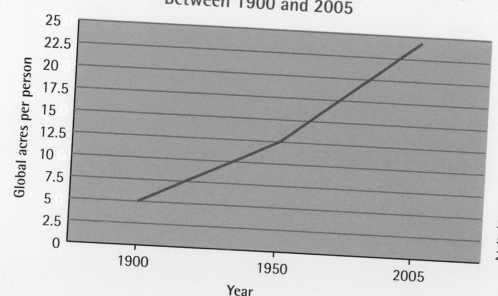

Increase in the Average Footprint in the United States Between 1900 and 2005

Global acres per person — 25, 22.5, 20, 17.5, 15, 12.5, 10, 7.5, 5, 2.5, 0

Year — 1900, 1950, 2005

### Fast Fact
People in the United States would need to reduce their consumption by more than 80 percent to live at sustainable levels.

*The size of the average footprint in the United States has increased from 5 global acres in 1900 to 24 global acres in 2005.*

9

# Toward a Sustainable Future: Comparing Resource Use and Reducing Demand

The ecological footprint measurement can be used to compare resource use across the world. It helps people understand how they can live more sustainably by reducing their resource demands.

## Ecological Footprints and Resource Use

Ecological footprints are important because they show where in the world resource use is greater than biocapacity. Comparing the ecological footprints of different lifestyles helps people understand the effects of their resource use.

### Human Impacts on Biocapacity

Ecological footprints also help highlight the effect of human activities on Earth's biocapacity. Human activity can change productive land into unproductive land. For example, poor farming practices can cause **land degradation**, such as **soil erosion** and **desertification**. Land also becomes unproductive when it is used for building cities and roads.

**Fast Fact**

In 2003, the estimated world biocapacity was 27.7 billion global acres. This is nearly one-quarter of the planet's surface.

*Unproductive land cannot be used to grow crops and support living things.*

When land is used for cities it is no longer considered productive.

## CASE STUDY
# Using Ecological Footprints

Mathis Wackernagel and William Rees are Canadian researchers. They were the first to write about ecological footprints. Using ecological footprints, they showed that the average Canadian lifestyle used about three times the amount of resources that Earth could provide.

## Defining Footprints

Wackernagel and Rees defined the term *ecological footprint* in 1992. They described it as the amount of land needed to produce everything people use and to absorb their waste.

## Productive Land

Wackernagel and Rees also calculated how much of the total area of Earth was productive land. A major difficulty was deciding which types of land are unproductive. For example, ice-covered land, the land cities are built on, and land degraded by desertification are unproductive.

### Fast Fact
The ecological footprint was first officially used in 2000 by the World Wildlife Fund. They used it in their Living Planet Report to measure human impacts on Earth.

# Increasing Carbon Footprints

A carbon footprint is part of an ecological footprint. It represents the amount of carbon dioxide that is emitted by people's activities. This includes burning fossil fuels for transportation and electricity. Carbon footprints make up about half of most large ecological footprints, and they are increasing.

## Calculating Carbon Footprints

Carbon footprints are calculated by estimating the biocapacity needed to absorb the carbon dioxide produced by people's activities. This biocapacity is required to prevent an increase of greenhouse gases in the atmosphere. It is estimated that about 0.86 global acres (0.35 global ha) of forest are needed to absorb a ton of carbon dioxide.

### Fast Fact
It is estimated that there are 27.7 billion acres of productive area on Earth. This is made up of about 22 billion global acres of land and 5.7 billion global acres of sea.

## Forest Clearing

Forest clearing releases large amounts of carbon dioxide into the atmosphere. Plants store carbon dioxide as they grow. After trees are cut down they are often burned or left to decay. This releases the carbon dioxide again, adding to carbon footprints.

*Power stations that burn coal to create electricity emit large amounts of carbon dioxide.*

This forest in Brazil has been cleared by burning.

## CASE STUDY
# Clearing Rain Forests in Brazil

Extensive areas of rain forest in Brazil are being cleared for crops. This is reducing the world's biocapacity and adding to carbon footprints.

## Brazil's Forests

Brazil contains one of the largest areas of tropical rain forest in the world. However, Brazil also has the highest rate of **deforestation** in the world. This is due to **timber harvesting** and forest clearing. Forest is being cleared to make room for the increasing population. It is also cleared to create farms for producing beef, soya beans, and corn.

## Forest Clearing for Biofuels

Forests are often cleared by burning. This releases carbon dioxide, adding to greenhouse gases. Today, forests are decreasing rapidly because they are being cleared to grow **biofuels**. In the past, these forest areas helped absorb the carbon dioxide released by burning fossil fuels.

### Fast Fact
Removal of large areas of rain forest also destroys the habitat of the plants and animals that live there. It reduces the rich biodiversity of rain forest systems.

13

# Toward a Sustainable Future: Reducing Carbon Footprints

People can reduce carbon footprints by cutting down their energy use. **Renewable energy**, including biofuels, can also be used to replace fossil fuels.

## Renewable Energy for Electricity

Renewable energy can replace fossil fuels for electricity production. For example, coal-fired power stations can be replaced with solar and wind power plants. Building these power plants still creates a carbon footprint, because resources are used to build the plants. However, their footprint is much smaller than the footprint of a coal-fired power station.

## Biofuels for Transportation

Biofuels can replace fossil fuels, such as oil, for transportation. Biofuels can be made from **biowaste** or from plants grown on land that is not good for growing food crops. This allows people to produce biofuels without clearing forests.

### Fast Fact
The world carbon footprint increased more than nine times between 1961 and 2003. This was mainly due to the increased use of fossil fuels.

*These wind turbines generate renewable energy for electricity when they are turned by the wind.*

Banners showing *Our Carbon Heroes* projects were displayed at a community event on World Environment Day in 2008.

## CASE STUDY

# Our Carbon Heroes

Our Carbon Heroes is a community project in central Victoria, Australia. It helps make people aware of how others are reducing carbon footprints. The project also celebrates the efforts of people who are reducing carbon footprints and tackling climate change.

## Knowing What to Change

Reducing footprints requires many lifestyle changes. Knowing what to change and how to change can be difficult. Switching off lights, growing food in the garden, and using **solar heating** are some of the changes people can make.

Our Carbon Heroes celebrates people's carbon-saving stories. The project uses art to inform individuals, communities, and governments about changes that work. Sharing people's stories within a community inspires other people to change as well.

### Fast Fact
It is estimated that preserving other living things requires at least 12 percent of the productive land on Earth. This needs to be included in footprint calculations if all life on Earth is to be protected.

# Unequal Shares of Resources

Many people across the world consume more resources than Earth can regenerate. At the same time, others are not getting the basic resources they need to survive.

## Footprint by Regions

Some regions of the world have large footprints due to high consumption of resources. Other regions have much smaller footprints because of a lack of resources. More than a billion people worldwide live with little or no access to sanitation, clean water, or health care.

**Fast Fact**
Today many areas in Asia have smaller footprints per person than developed countries. However, they do not necessarily have a poorer quality of life.

| Ecological Footprints Around the World ||
|---|---|
| **Region** | **Ecological footprint per person** |
| North America | 22.7 global acres |
| European Union | 11.6 global acres |
| Other parts of Europe | 8.6 global acres |
| Latin America and the Caribbean | 5.9 global acres |
| The Middle East and Central Asia | 5.7 global acres |
| Asia Pacific | 3.9 global acres |
| Africa | 2.7 global acres |

## Consumption and Quality of Life

A high-consumption lifestyle does not always result in a better quality of life. Many people in richer countries could reduce their footprints without lessening their quality of life.

*Many people in developed countries could reduce consumption through simple changes, such as walking or cycling instead of driving.*

Many people in Africa must walk to wells to collect water for their daily needs.

## CASE STUDY
# Small Shares of Resources

Most people in Africa use only a small share of the world's resources. The average African footprint is only 2.7 global acres (1.1 global ha) per person.

## Small Footprints, Slow Development

The small African footprints show slow development and very low standards of living. Many people do not have access to basic resources, such as clean water. Resources are also shared unequally among people. This has added to the number of people living in poverty.

## Africa's Decreasing Biocapacity

Africa's biocapacity is estimated at 3.2 global acres (1.3 global ha) per person. This is less than the world average. The land has been degraded by human activities, such as firewood harvesting and clearing of natural vegetation. Desertification is increasing as land is cleared and used too heavily by people. This has decreased the biocapacity of many areas.

### Fast Fact
In 1989, only nine trees were being replanted in Africa for every one hundred that were cut down. Since then, deforestation has caused serious problems, including soil erosion and water pollution.

17

# Toward a Sustainable Future: Increasing Access to Resources

Sustainable development strategies are being created in developed countries. These strategies can increase people's access to resources in the least developed areas of the globe. They are particularly needed across Africa and southern Asia.

## Peace and Health

An important step in sustainable development is maintaining peace and improving health. There are many ongoing **conflicts** in African countries, such as Liberia and Sudan. These conflicts can stand in the way of development. Health care, clean water, and sanitation are also vital to ensure a reasonable quality of life.

## Environmentally Friendly Development

Development also needs to be environmentally friendly, with programs to improve biocapacity. This can be done by replanting forests, improving soil conditions, and encouraging **low-tillage farming**. New buildings and houses can use renewable energy instead of fossil fuels.

### Fast Fact

In 2003, Earth's biocapacity was about 27.7 billion global acres. This is about 4.4 global acres per person. However, as the population increases and land degradation continues, the amount of biocapacity per person is decreasing.

*Solar panels can be used to provide renewable energy for villages in developing countries.*

*Workers employed by the Green Belt Movement have planted millions of trees in Kenya.*

CASE STUDY
# The Green Belt Movement

The Green Belt Movement of Kenya was founded by Wangari Maathai in 1977. It is a **nonprofit organization** working to improve the land in Kenya by planting trees.

## Planting Trees for the Environment

Green Belt has planted an estimated 20 million trees to help prevent soil erosion. The trees also provide firewood for cooking fires. Many women are employed to plant the trees. This provides them with money to help care for their children.

## Wangari Maathai

Wangari Maathai was born in 1940. She gained worldwide attention for speaking out against a luxury housing project in Kenya in 1998. The project would have led to the clearing of hundreds of acres of forest. She said, "No matter what problems wc face we can still protect the environment and think of future generations."

**Fast Fact**
Wangari Maathai was awarded the Nobel Peace Prize in 2003.

19

# Increasing National Footprints

Many scientists have warned that the need to reduce consumption is urgent. However, some nations have footprints that are still rapidly increasing.

## Luxury Lifestyles

A major part of increasing footprints is the luxury lifestyles of the rich in some countries. For example, large luxury houses often use energy inefficiently. Cheap and frequent flights are encouraging more and more air travel, which uses more fuel and increases carbon footprints.

## Luxury Housing

In cities such as Dubai (United Arab Emirates), Bombay (India), and Bangkok (Thailand), luxury apartments are replacing lower-cost homes. It is becoming harder for people with low incomes to afford housing. Luxury apartments are a good way of making a profit for developers, but they are disastrous for sustainability. They use a lot of energy and other resources.

*Airplanes burn large amounts of fossil fuels and emit a lot of carbon dioxide.*

**Fast Fact**
In 2005, Europe's ecological footprint in global acres was more than twice the size of the land in Europe.

Luxury developments, such as this community, are adding to the footprint in Dubai.

## CASE STUDY
# Luxury in Dubai

Dubai is a city in the United Arab Emirates (UAE). The UAE is an oil-rich desert country with very few other natural resources. Food must be imported, and water is provided mostly by removing the salt from seawater. This is called desalination. Food transportation and desalination both use fossil fuels, adding to very high energy consumption.

In 2007 the UAE's ecological footprint per person was the largest in the world, measuring 23.4 global acres (11.9 global ha). The world average was 5.4 global acres (2.2 global ha) per person.

## Rapid Construction in Dubai

Construction has been very rapid for some years in Dubai. The city now has many extremely luxurious developments. These include resort islands built over coral reefs and indoor snow skiing.

### Fast Fact
A 2007 footprint survey showed the United States had the second-largest footprint per person. Finland had the third largest and Canada the fourth largest.

# Toward a Sustainable Future: Limiting World Footprints

The nations of the world need to limit footprints while providing a reasonable standard of living for all people. Luxury lifestyles must be replaced by a more reasonable lifestyle that Earth can sustain.

## Calculating Sustainability

In 2007, the Global Footprint Network (GFN) calculated the sustainability of ninety-three nations. They used the countries' ecological footprints and the United Nations Human Development Index (HDI). The HDI measures life expectancy, literacy, levels of schooling, and economic wealth. It shows where there are inequalities. It also encourages developed countries to help developing countries, for example, by providing money for education programs.

## Maintaining Healthy Environments

Maintaining healthy natural environments is just as important as limiting footprints. These environments include forests, productive farmland, and fisheries.

### Fast Fact

The HDI rates countries' development with a score between zero and one. Scores near zero suggest that a country is not developing well. Developed countries have a score nearer to one.

*This Ugandan woman learned about sustainable farming methods through an education program funded by developed countries.*

22

In Cuba, people began to use bicycles for transportation because they did not have fuel for cars.

## CASE STUDY

# Cuba: A Sustainable Country

The Global Footprint Network's 2007 sustainability study found that Cuba is the only sustainable developed country in the world. The people of Cuba have a decent standard of living with a small, sustainable ecological footprint. This is mainly because of Cuba's low energy use.

## Cuban Self-Sufficiency

Cuba was forced to be self-sufficient from the 1990s. This was largely because the country was unable to import oil for political reasons. Without oil imports, Cuban people could not use tractors for farming. They started to grow local produce, developed natural pesticides and fertilizers, and reduced land tillage. They ate more locally grown fruits and vegetables. Since people did not have fuel for cars, they walked, rode bicycles, caught buses, and carpooled.

**Fast Fact**
Recent oil discoveries in Cuban waters could lead to an increase in Cuba's footprint.

The self-sufficient Cuban lifestyle uses fewer resources than any other equally developed country. Cuba provides a real-life model for other countries trying to achieve sustainable development.

# Ecological Overshoot

In late 1986, total human consumption began to exceed the biocapacity of Earth. Today it takes about one year and two months for Earth to regenerate what we use in one year. This debt is called ecological overshoot, and it is increasing each year.

## Dependence on Imports

Most countries already depend on imports from other countries to supply some of their needs. Many national footprints are greater than the biocapacity of their own country, leading to ecological overshoot. Regions with high **population densities** cannot produce enough to provide for their people. They import many of their resources, including coal, oil, and food, from all over the globe.

### Fast Fact

In 2008, Ecological Overshoot Day was September 23. This was the date when people had used the amount of resources Earth can regenerate in a single year. This means people used resources 40 percent faster than Earth was able to produce them.

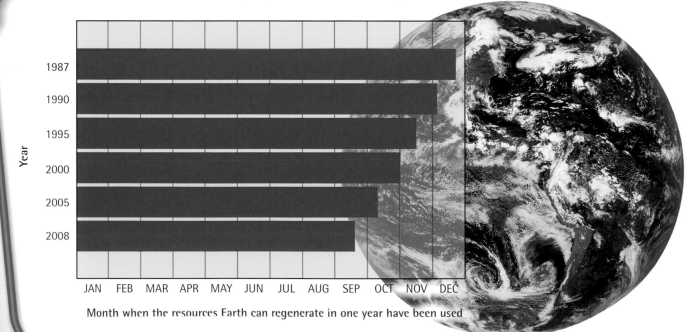

**Ecological Overshoot Day 1987–2008**

Year

1987
1990
1995
2000
2005
2008

JAN FEB MAR APR MAY JUN JUL AUG SEP OCT NOV DEC

Month when the resources Earth can regenerate in one year have been used

*Ecological Overshoot Day is getting earlier each year.*

Japan relies heavily on imports from other countries, as its people consume more than the land can provide.

## CASE STUDY

# High Population Density, Small Land Area

Japan has a high population density, but a very small land area. Its ecological footprint is larger than the biocapacity of its land. The resources used by Japanese people come mostly from outside Japan.

## Japan's Footprint

In 2005, Japan's footprint was 11.4 global acres (4.6 global ha) per person. This is a fairly low figure for a developed country, and is due to good use of land. In Tokyo, for example, land is used at several levels. In some areas, buildings extend for seven stories underground.

## Japan and Biocapacity

Even though Japan uses land well, its footprint is still larger than its biocapacity. This means that Japan cannot supply enough resources for the people who live there. The Japanese must import resources to provide for their needs.

**Fast Fact**
If the world's population grows as expected, by 2030 there will be 10 billion people on Earth. However, there will be an average of only 2.2 acres (0.9 ha) of productive land available per person.

# Toward a Sustainable Future: Living Within Earth's Limits

For a sustainable future all people must have access to a reasonable standard of living. However, we must also live within the limits of what Earth can provide.

## Controlling Population Growth

One of the main factors leading to the large world footprint is the large world population. Keeping population growth under control is a major challenge in the twenty-first century.

## Sustainable City Lifestyles

Today, more than half the world's people live in cities. We need to develop sustainable city lifestyles to avoid ecological overshoot. Using the renewable technologies that are already available and developing others can help produce a footprint that is within Earth's capacity.

*Recycling is one technology that is already available and can make city lifestyles more sustainable.*

GLASS, PLASTIC, CANS

**Fast Fact**

In Australia, a research organization is developing sustainable planning and design technologies. They hope to help people in cities cut their resource use by 20 percent by 2020.

## Composition of London's Ecological Footprint

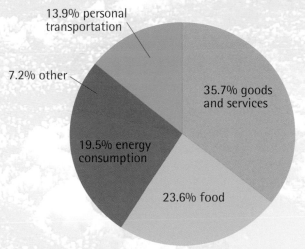

- 13.9% personal transportation
- 7.2% other
- 19.5% energy consumption
- 23.6% food
- 35.7% goods and services

*Most of London's ecological footprint comes from goods and services.*

*BedZED buildings are designed to help people reduce their ecological footprints.*

## CASE STUDY

# Remaking the City of London

In 2000, London's mayor began a detailed ecological footprint study to determine ways to remake the city.

## Reducing London's Footprint

In 2000, the ecological footprint of London was estimated to be 16.3 global acres (6.6 global ha) per person. This was 293 times the area of the city. London First and London Remade are two organizations that are working with businesses to drastically reduce London's footprint.

## Zero-Carbon Buildings

Many strategies are now being put in place across London, including zero-carbon buildings such as the Beddington Zero Energy Development (BedZED). This development combines many sustainable technologies. The buildings allow residents to produce their own energy, **recycle** waste, and collect rainwater. This reduces the costs of running the home and reduces the ecological footprint.

**Fast Fact**
London's 2012 Olympics are being described as the "One Planet Olympics." They will involve low-carbon and zero-waste strategies.

# What Can You Do?
## Reduce Your Own Footprint

All people need to consider how to reduce their own ecological footprint. Here are some suggestions on how to reduce your consumption in different parts of the footprint.

## Goods

- Be a careful consumer and only buy what you need.
- Buy recycled goods.
- Have damaged items repaired, when possible, rather than throwing them away.

## Waste

- Sort garbage to separate recycling and green waste.
- Reuse old things instead of throwing them away.

## Food

- Purchase foods that have not been transported long distances to get to you.
- Buy more local, in-season produce without packaging.

## Energy

- Switch off electrical appliances that are not in use.
- Open or close windows and doors to control the temperature in your home.
- Put on a sweater to keep warm rather than turning up the heat.

## Transportation

- Walk when possible.
- Use public transportation or carpool when possible.

*Repairing a broken appliance consumes fewer resources than would be needed to produce a new appliance.*

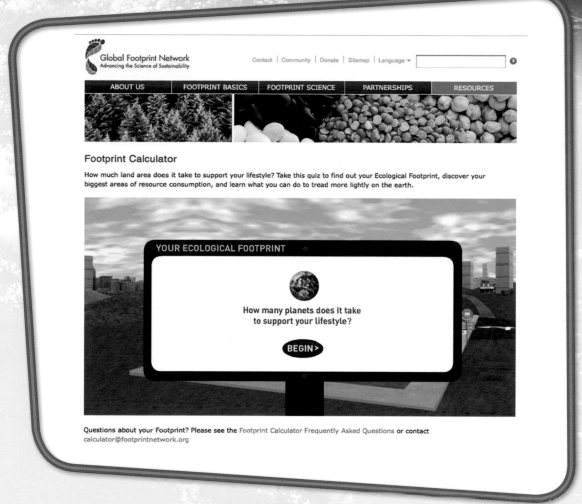

*You can take a footprint calculator quiz online.*

# Figure Out Your Carbon Footprint

You may not be able to choose renewable energy sources in your home and school. However, you can still reduce your own carbon footprint by reducing energy consumption. You can use an online calculator to figure out the size of your ecological footprint.

# Keep an Energy Savings Log

Keep a log of any energy savings that you make for one week, such as:

- switching off electrical appliances when they are not needed
- closing or opening curtains and windows to control the temperature in your house and reduce your use of air conditioning or heating
- choosing to walk or ride a bike rather than traveling by car for short trips
- putting on more clothes rather than turning up the heat

# Toward a Sustainable Future

**Well,** I hope you now see that if you take up my challenge your world will be a better place. There are many ways to work toward a sustainable future. Imagine a world with:

- a sustainable ecological footprint
- places of natural heritage protected for the future
- no more environmental pollution
- less greenhouse gas in the air, reducing global warming
- zero waste and efficient use of resources
- a secure food supply for all

This is what you can achieve if you work together with my natural systems.

We must work together to live sustainably. That will mean a better environment and a better life for all living things on Earth, now and in the future.

## Websites

For further information on ecological footprints, visit the following websites.

- Sustainable Development Partnerships www.sdp.gov
- London Remade www.londonremade.com
- Our Carbon Heroes www.focusoncommunity.org/OurCarbonHeroes.html
- Global Footprint Network www.footprintnetwork.org/en/index.php/GFN

# Glossary

**atmosphere**
The layers of gases surrounding Earth.

**biocapacity**
The area of land and sea which can produce food and other materials, and absorb waste.

**biofuels**
Fuels that are made from material produced by living things, such as corn or human waste.

**biowaste**
Waste from organic material, such as plant waste.

**carbon dioxide**
A colorless, odorless gas.

**conflicts**
Disagreements leading to battles or wars.

**consumption**
Amount used or consumed.

**deforestation**
Removal or clearing of forest cover.

**desertification**
Turning an area into desert, with low plant cover and a high risk of erosion.

**developed countries**
Countries with industrial development, a strong economy, and a high standard of living.

**emissions**
Substances released into the environment.

**fossil fuels**
Fuels such as oil, coal, and gas, which formed under the ground from the remains of animals and plants that lived millions of years ago.

**global warming**
An increase in the average temperature on Earth.

**greenhouse gases**
Gases that help trap heat in Earth's atmosphere.

**imported**
Brought into one country from another.

**land degradation**
A reduction in the quality or productivity of land.

**low-tillage farming**
Growing crops without plowing to disturb the soil as little as possible.

**nonprofit organization**
An organization that does not aim to make money.

**population densities**
The numbers of people living in different areas.

**recycle**
To reprocess a material so that it can be used again.

**renewable energy**
Energy from a source that can be constantly supplied and that does not run out, such as wind or the Sun.

**soil erosion**
The process of rock and soil being carried away by wind and water.

**solar heating**
Methods of heating that capture warmth directly from sunlight, rather than using solar panels.

**sustainable**
Does not use more resources than Earth can regenerate.

**timber harvesting**
Cutting down trees for wood.

# Index